THE ULTIMATE GUIDE TO DIGITAL TRANSFORMATION

How SMEs Can Innovate and Thrive

Cedric Yumba K

CONTENTS

INTRODUCTION

In today's economic landscape, digital transformation has become imperative for small and medium-sized enterprises (SMEs) seeking to remain competitive and thrive. With the rapid evolution of technology and increasing consumer expectations, SMEs must adapt to survive and seize new opportunities presented by the digital world.

This book aims to demystify the digital transformation process and provide a practical guide for SMEs. We will explore concrete strategies, essential tools, and real-life examples to help businesses at every stage of their digital journey. Whether you are just beginning your transformation or looking to optimize your current efforts, this guide is designed to help you navigate this constantly evolving landscape.

We will start with a deep understanding of what digital transformation is and why it is crucial for SMEs. Next, we will analyze the current state of your business through a digital SWOT assessment and an audit of your existing infrastructures and systems. We will also address the importance of company culture, the selection of appropriate technologies, and the digitization of business processes.

Finally, we will explore strategies to effectively engage your customers in the digital age and how to track and evaluate the progress made. Every SME has a unique journey in its digital transformation, and the goal of this book is to equip you with the knowledge and tools necessary to ensure the long-term growth and prosperity of your business.

Prepare to transform your SME and fully harness the benefits of the digital revolution. Welcome to the digital age!

CHAPTER 1: UNDERSTANDING DIGITAL TRANSFORMATION

To begin, it is essential to delve deeper to understand what this process truly involves. Digital transformation is not just about adopting new technologies; it encompasses a complete overhaul of business processes and company culture. In this chapter, we will explore the fundamentals of digital transformation, the key technologies that underpin it, and the profound impacts it can have on SMEs.

1.1 The Fundamentals of Digital Transformation

Digital transformation involves integrating digital technologies into all aspects of a business, fundamentally altering how it operates and delivers value to its customers. This process goes beyond simply adopting new technologies; it involves a complete rethinking of business processes, economic models, and company culture.

What is Digital Transformation?

Digital transformation refers to the changes associated with integrating digital technologies across all dimensions of a business. This includes:

- **Digitization**: Converting physical formats to digital formats (e.g., digitized paper documents).
- **Digitalization**: Using digital technologies to improve existing processes (e.g., adopting electronic document management systems).
- **Digital Transformation**: Rethinking and transforming processes, products, and business models through digital technologies (e.g., adopting a customer-centric strategy based on real-time data analysis).

Key Technologies

Certain technologies are fundamental to digital transformation and often represent the starting point of this process. Here are the most notable:

- **Cloud Computing**: Offers the ability to store and access data and applications on remote servers instead of relying on local infrastructure. This allows businesses to benefit from flexibility, scalability, and reduced operational costs.
- **Big Data**: Refers to the exploitation of large volumes of data to gain strategic insights. Collecting, analyzing, and interpreting this data allows businesses to better understand market trends, customer behaviors, and optimize their operations.
- **Internet of Things (IoT)**: Connects physical objects to

the internet, enabling data collection and exchange. IoT is used to improve process efficiency, such as inventory management, predictive maintenance, and task automation.
- **Artificial Intelligence (AI)**: Includes systems capable of simulating human processes such as learning and decision-making. AI is deployed to automate complex tasks, enhance customer service with chatbots, and perform predictive analyses.
- **Blockchain**: A decentralized ledger technology that secures and verifies transactions. Blockchain is used to ensure transparency and trust in sectors such as finance, supply chain management, and more.

Impacts on Business Processes and Economic Models

Digital transformation influences several functional and strategic aspects of SMEs:
- **Process Automation**: Digital technologies enable the automation of repetitive and labor-intensive tasks, freeing up time for higher-value activities and reducing human errors. For example, using software robots (RPA) for data entry or AI for email classification.
- **Improving Customer Experience**: Customer expectations evolve with technology. Businesses must now offer seamless, personalized, and real-time interactions. Adopting customer relationship management (CRM) platforms and data analytics helps SMEs better understand and meet customer needs.
- **New Economic Models**: Technologies enable the creation of innovative business models, such as online service platforms, subscription-based economies, or digital marketplaces. Companies can explore new revenue streams as a result.
- **Organizational Flexibility and Agility**: The adoption of remote work, facilitated by cloud computing and online collaboration tools, makes businesses more agile and responsive. They can quickly adjust their activities in

response to market changes.

In conclusion, an SME cannot afford to ignore digital transformation. Understanding its fundamentals and key technologies is essential to initiating this change, aligning business strategy with new digital realities, and fully capitalizing on them.

1.2 Why Digital Transformation is Crucial for SMEs

For small and medium-sized enterprises (SMEs), digital transformation is much more than mere modernization. It is essential for their survival and growth in an increasingly competitive and globalized market. This section explores the reasons why SMEs must embrace digital transformation.

Adapting to New Customer Expectations

Customer behaviors and expectations have evolved significantly with the rise of digital technologies. Customers now seek personalized, seamless, and rapid experiences. Key points include:

- **Responsiveness and Accessibility**: Customers expect to interact with businesses at any time and from any device. Adopting digital channels such as social media, mobile apps, and responsive websites has become crucial.
- **Personalization**: Through data analytics, SMEs can better understand their customers' preferences and offer tailored services and products. CRM and automated marketing tools play a key role in personalizing interactions and improving customer satisfaction.

Reducing Operational Costs

Digital transformation allows SMEs to significantly reduce costs and improve operational margins. Here's how:

- **Task Automation**: Digitalization allows for the automation of repetitive and manual processes, reducing the need for labor and minimizing errors associated with human intervention. For example, automating invoicing and payments.
- **Resource Optimization**: The use of ERP (Enterprise Resource Planning) systems helps optimize resource management, eliminating inefficiencies and improving coordination between different departments. SMEs can better plan and allocate their resources as a result.

- **Reducing Infrastructure Costs**: Migrating to the cloud allows businesses to reduce infrastructure costs, avoiding heavy investments in servers and reducing maintenance costs. They pay only for what they use.

Improving Decision-Making Through Data

Data plays a central role in digital transformation. Collecting and analyzing data enables SMEs to make more informed and strategic decisions. Several advantages result from this:

- **Data-Driven Insights**: Analyzing customer data, sales performance, and market trends provides valuable insights. Businesses can adapt their marketing strategies, optimize product offerings, and anticipate future needs as a result.
- **Real-Time Monitoring**: Digital technologies offer the ability to monitor operations in real-time. Analytical dashboards and business intelligence tools allow for the tracking of key performance indicators (KPIs) and quick responses to anomalies or opportunities.
- **Prediction and Planning**: Predictive analytics tools use machine learning algorithms to forecast future trends and plan accordingly. For example, predicting seasonal demand to manage inventory more effectively.

In conclusion, digital transformation offers SMEs a unique opportunity to modernize, streamline operations, and better meet customer expectations. Ignoring this transformation poses a significant risk, as companies that do not adopt digital technologies can quickly be overtaken by more agile and innovative competitors. Digital transformation is therefore not just a growth strategy but a necessary condition for the survival and success of SMEs in the modern economy.

CHAPTER 2: ASSESSING THE CURRENT STATE OF YOUR SME

Now that we have a clear understanding of what digital transformation is, the next step is to assess the current state of your business. Before you can develop an effective strategy, it is crucial to know your strengths and weaknesses, as well as the opportunities and threats you face. This chapter will guide you through a digital SWOT analysis and an audit of your existing infrastructures and systems, providing a solid foundation for planning your digital transformation.

2.1 Digital SWOT Analysis (Strengths, Weaknesses, Opportunities, Threats)

The SWOT (Strengths, Weaknesses, Opportunities, Threats) analysis is a valuable strategic tool for evaluating your company's current state in the context of digital transformation. This method allows you to identify your internal strengths and weaknesses as well as external opportunities and threats. Applying this analysis to your digital landscape provides a clear vision for planning your next steps.

How to Conduct a SWOT Analysis

To perform a digital SWOT analysis, follow these steps:

1. **Form a Multidisciplinary Team**: Bring together members from different departments to get a comprehensive view of the company.
2. **Collect Data**: Gather information from various sources such as financial reports, customer feedback, technology audits, and market analyses.
3. **Organize Brainstorming Sessions**: Use collaborative workshops to list your strengths, weaknesses, opportunities, and threats.
4. **Prioritize Elements**: Rank each item in order of priority to focus your efforts on the most critical points.
5. **Document and Communicate**: Formalize the results of your analysis in a document shared with the entire team.

Interpreting the Results

Once your digital SWOT analysis is complete, it's time to interpret it and use it to guide your digital strategy.

- **Strengths**: Identify your SME's digital assets. This may include a robust technological infrastructure, a skilled IT team, or already digitized processes. Leverage these strengths to build your digital transformation strategy.
- **Weaknesses**: Identify the weak points that could hinder your digital transformation. For example, reliance on

outdated systems, lack of digital skills among staff, or resistance to change. Weaknesses should be addressed quickly to avoid compromising your efforts.

- **Opportunities**: Identify external opportunities that can accelerate your digital transformation. This includes market trends, technological advancements, government subsidies, or new market segments. Exploit these opportunities to increase your competitiveness and generate new revenue streams.
- **Threats**: Assess external threats that may challenge your digital transformation, such as increased competition, cyber threats, regulatory changes, or economic disruptions. Prepare contingency plans to mitigate these risks.

A digital SWOT analysis provides a clear mapping of your company's current state and helps set strategic priorities. By combining this analysis with an in-depth audit of your existing infrastructures and systems, you can develop a precise roadmap for your digital transformation, aligned with your strengths and opportunities, while anticipating and mitigating your weaknesses and threats.

2.2 Audit of Existing Infrastructures and Systems

An audit of existing infrastructures and systems is an essential step to understand the current state of your digital transformation. It allows you to better assess your technological capabilities, identify gaps, and set priorities for necessary upgrades. A well-conducted audit provides a solid foundation for planning your digital roadmap.

Evaluating Current Systems

To begin the audit, it is important to thoroughly examine the key components of your technological infrastructure:

- **Inventory of Hardware Equipment**: Create a comprehensive list of all IT equipment, including servers, computers, network peripherals, and storage devices. Note the condition, age, and performance of each item.
- **Inventory of Software and Applications**: Compile an inventory of the software in use, including operating systems, business applications, productivity tools, and security solutions. Check versions and licenses to ensure they are up to date.
- **Networks and Connectivity**: Analyze your network configuration, including routers, switches, bandwidth, and security protocols. Evaluate reliability, speed, and potential vulnerabilities.
- **Data Storage and Management**: Assess your data storage systems, checking their capacity, efficiency, and redundancy levels. Also, consider your data backup and recovery practices to ensure business continuity.
- **Security Systems**: Review your current security measures, such as firewalls, antivirus software, intrusion detection systems, and access management policies. Identify security gaps and areas needing improvement.

Identifying Needs and Priorities

After detailing the current state, it's time to identify needs and prioritize improvements. Focus on areas that will have the greatest impact on your productivity, security, and ability to innovate. Here are some key steps to achieve this:

- **Strategic Alignment Analysis**: Ensure that your current infrastructure supports your strategic goals. For example, if your vision includes expanding into e-commerce, check that your systems can handle increased online traffic and secure transactions.
- **Technology Gap Assessment**: Compare your current infrastructure with industry standards and best practices. Identify significant gaps and assess their potential impact on your operations.
- **Upgrade Planning**: Develop a plan to improve or replace outdated systems and strengthen weak components. Prioritize upgrades based on their urgency and strategic impact.
- **Budget and Resource Estimation**: Evaluate the costs associated with upgrades and plan the necessary resources, including budgets, timelines, and required technical skills.

Conclusion of the Audit

The conclusion of your audit should result in a detailed report summarizing findings and prioritizing actions. This report will serve as the basis for developing your digital transformation strategy, providing you with a clear and concrete view of your current technological state and the necessary improvements.

With a comprehensive audit of existing infrastructures and systems, your SME will be better prepared to confidently and knowledgeably approach the next stages of digital transformation.

CHAPTER 3: DEVELOPING A DIGITAL TRANSFORMATION STRATEGY

With a comprehensive assessment of your current state in hand, it's time to define a clear vision and measurable goals for your digital transformation. A well-thought-out strategy is essential to guide your business through the many stages of this process. This chapter will show you how to define an inspiring vision, set SMART goals, engage stakeholders, and form a dedicated team to ensure the success of your transformation.

3.1 Defining a Clear Vision and Goals

Defining a clear vision and measurable goals is a crucial step in successfully achieving your SME's digital transformation. A well-articulated vision inspires and guides the entire company, while specific goals allow for measuring progress and staying on track.

Importance of the Vision

The vision for digital transformation should be an inspiring statement that captures the essence of what you want to achieve. It should reflect your company's long-term ambition regarding digitalization. A good vision should:

- **Align with the overall business strategy**: The digital vision must complement your SME's mission and core values.
- **Encourage engagement across the company**: It should motivate and inspire employees, customers, and partners.
- **Serve as a guide in decision-making**: A clear vision helps steer strategic and operational choices.

Example of a vision: "To become a leader in our industry by leveraging digital technologies to deliver exceptional customer experiences and optimize our internal processes."

How to Set Measurable Goals

Once the vision is defined, it is crucial to set specific, measurable, achievable, realistic, and time-bound (SMART) goals. Here's how to proceed:

- **Specific**: Goals should be clear and precise. Avoid generalities. For example, "Increase online sales by 20% by the end of the year" is more specific than "Improve online sales."
- **Measurable**: Ensure that each goal can be quantified. Use key performance indicators (KPIs) to track progress and measure success. For example, "Reduce order processing time to less than 24 hours."
- **Achievable**: Goals should be attainable with the resources available. Consider your team's capabilities

and budget constraints. For example, "Train 100% of staff on new technologies within six months" is achievable with an adequate training plan.

- **Realistic**: Goals should be relevant to your company's current situation and strategic priorities. Avoid setting overly ambitious or unrealistic goals. For example, "Launch a new e-commerce platform within six months" is realistic if you have the necessary resources.
- **Time-bound**: Set a deadline for each goal. This creates a sense of urgency and helps maintain focus. For example, "Migrate all data to the cloud by June 30."

Goal-Setting Process

To set SMART goals, follow these steps:

1. **Needs and Opportunities Analysis**: Based on the digital audit and SWOT analysis, identify priority areas for your digital transformation.
2. **Stakeholder Consultation**: Engage key internal and external stakeholders to gather insights and recommendations.
3. **Action Plan Development**: Break down each goal into specific tasks with assigned responsibilities and precise deadlines.
4. **Monitoring Mechanisms**: Use project management tools and dashboards to track progress and adjust plans if necessary.

By defining an inspiring vision and clear, measurable goals, your SME will be able to confidently navigate the path of digital transformation. This creates a compelling roadmap that mobilizes resources and ensures strategic alignment at every stage of the process.

3.2 Engaging Stakeholders and Forming a Dedicated Team

To ensure the success of your SME's digital transformation, it is essential to engage stakeholders and form a dedicated team. This helps to mobilize the necessary resources, foster buy-in for the project, and ensure that all required skills are available.

Identifying and Engaging Stakeholders

Stakeholders are all the people or groups who can influence or be influenced by digital transformation. Identifying and effectively engaging them is crucial to facilitate the implementation of your strategy.

- **Who are the stakeholders?**
    - **Internal**: Leaders, managers, employees, IT, operations, finance, marketing departments, etc.
    - **External**: Suppliers, customers, technology partners, consultants, investors.
- **How to engage stakeholders?**
    - **Communicate the vision and goals**: Clearly share the strategic vision and goals of digital transformation with all stakeholders.
    - **Gather feedback**: Encourage stakeholders to express their concerns, ideas, and expectations. Organize meetings, surveys, and workshops to promote open dialogue.
    - **Assign roles and responsibilities**: Clearly define each stakeholder's role in the project. Assign specific responsibilities to ensure their engagement and contribution.

Formation and Role of the Dedicated Team

Establishing a dedicated digital transformation team is a critical step in consistently and effectively leading and coordinating the project.

- **Composition of the dedicated team**: The team should be multidisciplinary, bringing together the varied skills necessary for the success of digital transformation.

- **Project Manager**: Responsible for overall coordination, resource management, and overseeing timelines.
- **IT Experts**: Handle technical implementation, systems integration, and management of technological infrastructures.
- **Data Analysts**: Specialize in data collection, analysis, and interpretation to inform strategic decisions.
- **Business Leaders**: Representatives from different departments to align digital initiatives with specific operational needs.
- **Communication Specialists**: Ensure smooth and transparent communication around the project, both internally and externally.

- **Roles and responsibilities of the dedicated team**:
  - **Planning and Coordination**: Develop a project timeline, assign tasks, and ensure that milestones are met.
  - **Monitoring and Evaluation**: Track progress, measure performance against defined KPIs, and adjust plans if necessary.
  - **Training and Support**: Provide ongoing training to develop employees' digital skills and offer technical support.
  - **Change Management**: Identify resistance to change and implement strategies to overcome it, such as awareness programs or incentives for adopting new technologies.

Team Formation Process

To form an effective dedicated team, follow these steps:

1. **Internal and External Recruitment**: Determine the required skills and recruit accordingly. You can train existing staff members or hire new talent.
2. **Team Structure Development**: Define a clear structure with precise roles and well-established lines of

responsibility.

3. **Training Plan Development**: Identify training needs and develop programs to enhance the team's skills.

4. **Communication Mechanisms**: Establish effective communication channels to facilitate coordination and collaboration within the team and with external stakeholders.

By methodically engaging stakeholders and forming a high-potential dedicated team, your SME will maximize its chances of successfully achieving digital transformation. This approach ensures smooth management, better synergy between different actors, and guarantees that all aspects of the transformation are duly considered and managed.

3.3 Developing a Detailed Roadmap

To effectively navigate digital transformation, a detailed roadmap is fundamental. It structures initiatives, sets priorities, and tracks progress throughout the process. A well-designed roadmap ensures that each stage of the transformation is planned coherently and realistically.

Creating an Action Plan

The first step in developing a roadmap is to create a detailed action plan. This plan should include all the initiatives, projects, and activities necessary to achieve your digital goals.

- **Project Phasing**: Divide digital transformation into distinct phases, each with specific objectives. For example: initial assessment, preparation, implementation, and optimization.
- **Task Detailing**: List all the tasks required for each phase, from the smallest to the most complex. Ensure that each task is well-defined and understandable.
- **Resource Requirements**: Identify the human, technological, and financial resources needed for each task. Allocate budgets for software, hardware, training, etc.
- **Dependencies and Sequencing**: Note dependencies between tasks and organize them in a logical sequential order to avoid bottlenecks and blockages.

Establishing a Realistic Timeline

A realistic timeline is essential for the effective implementation of your roadmap. It helps keep the project on track and avoid undue delays.

- **Deadline Setting**: Set precise deadlines for each task and phase of the project. Be realistic about the time required for each activity, considering possible contingencies.
- **Milestone Setting**: Identify key milestones throughout the project. These milestones are important checkpoints to assess progress and adjust plans if necessary.
- **Workload Distribution**: Ensure that the workload

is well distributed among team members. Avoid overloading certain individuals and make efficient use of all available skills.

- **Contingency Management**: Include safety margins in the timeline to manage unforeseen events or potential delays. Prepare contingency plans for identified risks.

Monitoring and Adjusting the Plan

To ensure that your roadmap remains relevant and effective throughout the project, it is crucial to establish continuous monitoring and adjustment mechanisms.

- **Tracking Tools**: Use project management tools to track the progress of tasks and phases. Software like Trello, Asana, or Microsoft Project can be useful in maintaining organization.
- **Performance Measurement**: Regularly assess progress using defined KPIs. For example, monitor task completion rates, costs versus budget, and timelines versus schedule.
- **Periodic Reviews**: Hold regular meetings to assess the project's status. These meetings provide opportunities to share progress, resolve issues, and make quick decisions to adjust the plan if necessary.
- **Continuous Feedback**: Encourage continuous feedback from stakeholders and team members. Use these insights to improve and adapt the roadmap along the way.

Finalizing the Roadmap

When finalizing the roadmap, ensure that it is well-documented and shared with all relevant stakeholders. This includes communicating deadlines, milestones, responsibilities, and expectations. Good visibility and transparency around the roadmap facilitate buy-in and engagement from the entire team.

By developing a detailed and realistic roadmap, your SME will have a clear strategic plan to effectively manage digital transformation. This approach will coordinate efforts, maximize resource use, and track progress toward achieving set goals.

CHAPTER 4: CHANGING THE CORPORATE CULTURE

Strategy alone is not enough to achieve a successful digital transformation; corporate culture plays an equally crucial role. The transition to a digital organization requires adapting mindsets and behaviors at all levels of the company. In this chapter, we will discuss ways to raise awareness and train employees, encourage innovation and agility, and manage change while overcoming resistance.

4.1 Raising Awareness and Training Employees

The success of an SME's digital transformation largely depends on the engagement and competence of its employees. Training and sensitizing them to new technologies and organizational changes is essential to ensure a smooth and efficient transition.

The Importance of Continuous Training

Investing in continuous employee training helps keep skills up-to-date and ensures quick adaptation to new technologies and processes. Here's why it's crucial:

- **Adaptability to New Technologies**: Technologies are constantly evolving. Continuous training keeps employees competent and productive in the face of these changes.
- **Reduction of Resistance**: Well-trained and informed employees are generally less resistant to change, as they understand the benefits and feel more confident in their abilities.
- **Improved Performance**: Mastery of digital tools enhances work efficiency and quality, leading to better overall company performance.

Awareness Programs

Raising awareness is the first step in preparing employees for digital transformation. It must be well-planned and executed to maximize impact.

- **Information Campaigns**: Use internal platforms, newsletters, posters, and meetings to inform employees about digital transformation and its benefits for the company and themselves.
- **Awareness Workshops**: Organize interactive workshops where employees can ask questions and receive direct answers. These sessions also help dispel fears and clarify misunderstandings.
- **Testimonials and Case Studies**: Invite experts or representatives from other companies who have successfully undergone digital transformation. Their

testimonials can inspire and convince your employees of the importance of the project.

Developing Digital Skills

Employee training should be structured and tailored to the specific needs of the company and its employees.

- **Assessment of Current Skills**: Start with an assessment of your employees' current digital skills. This helps identify gaps and design targeted training.
- **Customized Training Plan**: Develop training plans tailored to different skill levels and employee roles. Training can cover topics such as specific software use, data management, cybersecurity, and online work practices.
- **Hands-On Training**: Prioritize practical and interactive training that allows employees to immediately apply what they've learned. Use simulations, live demonstrations, and practical exercises.
- **Use of E-Learning Platforms**: E-learning platforms offer the flexibility for employees to train at their own pace. These platforms often provide interactive modules, quizzes, and certifications.

Encouraging Autonomy and Self-Training

In addition to formal training, encourage employees to take charge of their learning and continue training autonomously.

- **Access to Online Resources**: Provide access to online resources such as video tutorials, articles, webinars, and discussion forums.
- **Creation of Communities of Practice**: Encourage employees to share their knowledge and experiences through discussion groups, tech book clubs, or regular meetings. These communities can be an excellent way to disseminate best practices and promote collective learning.
- **Recognition and Incentives**: Recognize and reward employees who show significant progress in their digital skills or actively encourage their colleagues to

train. Incentives can include certifications, bonuses, or professional development opportunities.

By raising awareness and training your employees, you not only prepare them to adapt to the changes brought about by digital transformation but also actively involve them in the process. This enhances their engagement and motivation, facilitating a successful and sustainable transition for your SME.

4.2 Encouraging Innovation and Agility

For a successful digital transformation, it is crucial to create an environment that fosters innovation and agility within your SME. Encouraging employees to innovate and adopt agile methodologies accelerates transformation processes, allows for quicker adaptation to changes, and effectively responds to market needs.

Creating an Environment Conducive to Innovation

An environment conducive to innovation stimulates creativity and experimentation, allowing employees to propose new ideas and test them.

- **Culture of Experimentation**: Encourage a culture that values experimentation and does not fear failure. Allow employees to try new ideas without the fear of negative repercussions in case of failure. Learn from each experience to improve processes.
- **Encouragement of Ideas**: Implement programs such as idea boxes, hackathons, or innovation contests where employees can submit and present their proposals. Reward the most innovative ideas and implement them.
- **Training in Creativity and Innovation**: Offer workshops and training on creative techniques, design thinking, and problem-solving methods. These skills can help employees formulate and develop innovative ideas.

Adopting Agile Methodologies

Agile methodologies enable your company to adapt quickly to changes, improve collaboration, and optimize the execution of digital projects.

- **Agile Principles**: Adopt agile principles such as rapid iteration, close team collaboration, flexibility, and customer orientation. These principles promote increased responsiveness and better adaptation to market needs.
- **Scrum and Kanban**: Use agile frameworks like Scrum

and Kanban to structure your projects. Scrum focuses on sprints, or short work cycles, with regular reviews to adjust priorities. Kanban visualizes workflow and allows for real-time workload management.

- **Cross-Functional Teams**: Create autonomous cross-functional teams capable of working on projects independently. These teams should include diverse skills such as development, UX design, marketing, and project management.

Encouraging Collaborative Innovation

Innovation should not be confined to a single team or department. Encouraging inter-departmental collaboration and involving external stakeholders can enrich the innovation process.

- **Collaborative Brainstorming Sessions**: Organize regular inter-departmental brainstorming sessions to generate ideas and solve problems. Use techniques like mind mapping or Lean Startup to structure these sessions.
- **External Partnerships**: Collaborate with startups, universities, incubators, and other external actors to benefit from new perspectives and complementary skills. These partnerships can accelerate innovation by introducing new ideas and technologies.
- **Online Collaboration Platforms**: Use online collaboration platforms to facilitate idea exchange and cooperation among employees, even remotely. Tools like Slack, Trello, or Microsoft Teams can improve communication and project management.

Tracking and Evaluating Innovation

To make innovation an integral part of your business, it is essential to continuously track and evaluate innovative initiatives.

- **Innovation KPIs**: Set key performance indicators (KPIs) to track innovation, such as the number of ideas generated, the implementation rate of new ideas, or the return on investment of innovative projects.

- **Feedback and Continuous Improvement**: Establish regular feedback mechanisms to evaluate innovative initiatives and continuously improve. Use the lessons learned to refine your processes and encourage even more effective innovation.
- **Celebrating Success**: Recognize and celebrate innovative successes. Whether through rewards, public recognition, or promotions, valuing successes reinforces employee engagement and stimulates further innovation.

By encouraging innovation and agility, you create a dynamic and resilient corporate culture, ready to tackle the challenges of digital transformation. This enables your SME to stay competitive, anticipate market changes, and generate sustainable growth.

4.3 Managing Change and Overcoming Resistance

Change management is one of the most delicate components of digital transformation. Resistance to change is common, but it can be overcome with a strategic and empathetic approach. This subchapter explores techniques for effectively managing change and minimizing resistance.

Change Management Strategies

To facilitate the digital transformation process, it is essential to implement well-defined change management strategies.

- **Transparent Communication**: Regularly inform employees about the reasons, benefits, and steps of the change. Open communication reduces uncertainties and builds trust. Use various channels like meetings, emails, internal dashboards, and discussion forums to disseminate information.
- **Engaged Leadership**: The support of leaders is crucial to legitimize the change. Leaders should embody the change, set an example, and be accessible to address employees' questions and concerns. Visible and active leadership strengthens the project's credibility.
- **Participatory Planning**: Involve employees in planning the change. Seek their ideas and feedback through workshops, surveys, and working groups. This participatory approach increases buy-in and provides valuable insights for refining strategies.

Techniques for Overcoming Resistance

Resistance to change can take various forms, ranging from legitimate concerns to recalcitrant behaviors. Use these techniques to overcome them:

- **Early Identification of Resistance**: Be proactive in detecting signs of resistance. Observe behaviors, listen to feedback, and anticipate potential challenges by conducting anonymous surveys or holding open meetings.

- **Training and Psychological Support**: Offer training sessions to develop the necessary skills and alleviate fears related to the unknown. Additionally, provide psychological support to help employees manage stress and anxiety associated with change.
- **Change Champions**: Designate "change champions" among influential employees who fully support digital transformation. These champions can motivate their colleagues, share positive experiences, and act as intermediaries between management and the rest of the team.
- **Process Adaptation**: Be flexible and willing to adjust processes based on employee feedback. For example, if a new technology or process encounters significant resistance, reassess its implementation and explore less disruptive alternatives.

Incentives and Recognition

Incentives and recognition play a key role in encouraging change adoption and maintaining employee motivation.

- **Material and Immaterial Incentives**: Offer material incentives (bonuses, promotions) and immaterial incentives (public recognition, development opportunities) to reward employees' efforts and engagement in digital transformation.
- **Celebrating Success**: Organize events to celebrate successes, whether it's completing a project phase, adopting a new tool, or achieving set objectives. This recognition reinforces motivation and team spirit.
- **Constructive Feedback**: Provide constructive and regular feedback. Acknowledge individual and collective efforts, and offer suggestions for improvement to maintain the momentum of change.

Continuous Evaluation and Adjustment

Change management is a dynamic process that requires continuous evaluation and adjustment.

- **Monitoring Progress**: Use performance indicators to track the progress of digital transformation initiatives and measure the impact of change on the organization. Satisfaction surveys, training assessments, and activity reports are useful tools in this regard.
- **Adjusting Strategies**: Based on results and employee feedback, adjust change management strategies. Be ready to recalibrate plans, reallocate resources, and modify methodologies to better meet the needs of the company and its employees.
- **Organizational Learning**: Foster an environment of continuous learning where lessons learned are shared and integrated into future practices. This strengthens organizational resilience and prepares the company to better manage subsequent changes.

By implementing well-planned change management strategies and addressing resistance with empathy and pragmatism

CHAPTER 5: IMPLEMENTING DIGITAL TECHNOLOGIES

Once your corporate culture is aligned with your digital vision, it's time to focus on implementing the right technologies. Choosing the right tools and technological solutions is crucial for modernizing your processes and improving operational efficiency. This chapter explores various technological options, from customer relationship management (CRM) systems to cloud migration, as well as IT security and data protection.

5.1 Choosing the Right Technological Solutions (CRM, ERP, Collaborative Tools, etc.)

Selecting the right technological solutions for your SME is a crucial step in the digital transformation process. The tools you choose must not only meet the current needs of the business but also be flexible enough to adapt to future changes. This subchapter explores how to select and implement key technological solutions like CRM, ERP, and collaborative tools.

Criteria for Selecting Tools

To choose the right technological solutions, it is important to consider several criteria:

- **Specific Business Needs**: Start by analyzing your specific needs. Which processes do you want to improve or automate? What are the gaps in your current systems?
- **Scalability**: The solutions should be able to grow with your business. Ensure that the software can handle an increase in data volume, users, and transactions.
- **Integration**: Technologies should integrate easily with your existing systems. Good integration minimizes disruptions and simplifies workflows.
- **Ease of Use**: The tools should be intuitive and easy for all staff to use. A user-friendly interface accelerates adoption and reduces training needs.
- **Total Cost of Ownership**: Evaluate not only the initial purchase and implementation costs but also recurring costs like subscriptions, maintenance, and updates.
- **Security and Compliance**: Ensure that the solutions meet the relevant security and compliance standards for your industry. Protecting sensitive data and information is paramount.

Overview of Key Available Solutions

- **CRM (Customer Relationship Management)**

CRM is essential for managing customer relationships, optimizing sales, and improving customer satisfaction.

- **Key Features**: Contact management, customer interaction tracking, opportunity management, sales automation, analytics, and reporting.
- **Examples of Solutions**: Salesforce, HubSpot CRM, Zoho CRM, Microsoft Dynamics 365.
- **Benefits for SMEs**: Better customer understanding, effective sales tracking, personalized interactions, and improved customer loyalty.

- **ERP (Enterprise Resource Planning)**

ERP centralizes various business functions such as accounting, human resources, production, and procurement into an integrated system.

- **Key Features**: Financial management, supply chain management, human resource management, production management, reporting, and analytics.
- **Examples of Solutions**: SAP Business One, Oracle NetSuite, Odoo, Microsoft Dynamics 365 Finance and Operations.
- **Benefits for SMEs**: Data centralization, reduced information silos, improved operational efficiency, and better decision-making through consolidated data.

- **Collaborative Tools**

Collaborative tools facilitate communication and cooperation between teams, especially in remote or geographically dispersed work environments.

- **Key Features**: Instant messaging, project management, document sharing, video conferencing, shared dashboards.
- **Examples of Solutions**: Microsoft Teams, Slack, Trello, Asana, Google Workspace.
- **Benefits for SMEs**: Improved internal communication, increased productivity, easier project coordination, and real-time collaboration.

Implementation Process

Once solutions are selected, their implementation must be

planned and executed in a structured manner.

- **Evaluation of Current Processes**: Analyze current processes to identify bottlenecks and areas for improvement. Use this information to properly configure the new solutions.
- **Implementation Planning**: Develop a detailed plan including implementation steps, team responsibilities, timelines, and required resources.
- **User Training**: Organize training sessions to familiarize employees with the new technologies. Ensure that training covers key features and best practices.
- **Testing and Adjustments**: Before full deployment, conduct tests to verify that the systems work as expected. Gather user feedback and make necessary adjustments.
- **Deployment and Support**: Roll out the solution company-wide and provide ongoing technical support to resolve issues and help users adapt.

By choosing and implementing the right technological solutions, your SME can optimize its processes, improve customer satisfaction, and stay competitive in a constantly evolving digital environment.

5.2 Cloud Migration and Data Management

Migrating to the cloud is a key step in the digital transformation of SMEs. This transition offers increased flexibility, better data management, and significant cost savings. This section discusses the benefits of cloud computing, the steps for a successful migration, and best practices for managing data in the cloud.

Benefits of Cloud Computing

Cloud computing offers several major benefits for SMEs:

- **Flexibility and Scalability**: The cloud allows you to easily adjust resources according to business needs, whether to increase or decrease storage and processing capacities.
- **Cost Reduction**: By eliminating significant initial investments in hardware and transferring maintenance costs to cloud service providers, SMEs can achieve significant savings.
- **Accessibility**: Data and applications hosted in the cloud are accessible at any time and from anywhere, facilitating remote work and collaboration.
- **Security and Compliance**: Cloud service providers invest in advanced security solutions and often adhere to compliance standards, ensuring the protection of sensitive data.
- **Automatic Updates**: Cloud services are regularly updated with the latest features and patches, avoiding disruptions and costs associated with manual updates.

Steps for a Successful Migration

Migrating to the cloud requires careful planning and rigorous execution. Here are the essential steps for a successful transition:

1. **Initial Assessment**:
   - **Needs Analysis**: Identify the applications and data to migrate, determining their criticality and specific requirements.
   - **Choosing the Cloud Model**: Decide on the appropriate deployment type for your SME

(public, private, hybrid) based on security, performance, and cost needs.

2. **Migration Planning**:
   - **Roadmap**: Develop a detailed roadmap including migration phases, team responsibilities, and timelines.
   - **Resource Allocation**: Assign the necessary human and technical resources to execute the plan, potentially including external partners or consultants.

3. **Data Preparation**:
   - **Data Cleanup**: Remove redundant and obsolete data to reduce the volume to be migrated and improve data quality.
   - **Data Security**: Encrypt sensitive data before migration to ensure its security during transfer.

4. **Migration Execution**:
   - **Migration Testing**: Perform test migrations in development environments to identify and resolve potential issues before migrating data to production.
   - **Gradual Migration**: Migrate applications and data in stages, starting with less critical components to minimize risks.

5. **Validation and Optimization**:
   - **Validation Testing**: Verify the integrity and performance of migrated data and applications to ensure they function as expected.
   - **Optimization of Configurations**: Adjust cloud configurations based on performance and business needs, optimizing costs and efficiency.

Data Management in the Cloud

Once data is migrated to the cloud, effective management is crucial to ensure security, compliance, and availability.

- **Data Governance Policies**: Establish clear policies for data management, including security responsibilities, access controls, and regulatory compliance.

- **Backup and Recovery**: Implement robust backup solutions and disaster recovery processes to protect data from loss and interruptions.
- **Performance Monitoring and Management**: Use monitoring tools to track the performance of cloud applications and data. Identify bottlenecks and make necessary adjustments.
- **Cost Control**: Monitor cloud resource consumption and optimize configurations to avoid unnecessary expenses. Take advantage of flexible pricing options like reserved instances or spot instances to reduce costs.
- **Ongoing Training**: Ensure that employees are trained in best practices for cloud data management and understand security and compliance procedures.

By migrating to the cloud and optimizing data management, your SME will benefit from a flexible and secure infrastructure capable of meeting the evolving needs of the business and supporting sustainable growth.

5.3 IT Security and Data Protection

IT security and data protection are critical components of digital transformation for any SME. It is imperative to implement robust measures to protect sensitive data from cyber threats and ensure compliance with relevant regulations. This subchapter explores the main security threats, best practices for securing systems and data, and solutions to ensure the continuous protection of information.

Key Threats and Vulnerabilities

SMEs are particularly vulnerable to cyberattacks due to often limited resources for defense. Here are some of the main threats:

- **Malware**: Viruses, worms, Trojans, and ransomware can infect systems, steal data, or render files inaccessible.
- **Phishing and Social Engineering**: Phishing attacks exploit employee trust to obtain sensitive information or introduce malware.
- **Denial of Service Attacks (DDoS)**: These attacks aim to make online services unavailable by overwhelming servers with requests.
- **Internal Security Breaches**: Human errors, inappropriate permissions, and incorrect configurations can create vulnerabilities exploited by cybercriminals.
- **Lack of Updates**: Unpatched software can contain known security vulnerabilities that attackers use to access systems.

Best Practices for Securing Data

To effectively protect your systems and data, implement the following security best practices:

- **Network Security**: Use firewalls, intrusion detection and prevention systems (IDS/IPS), and VPNs to secure network communications and protect the company's perimeter.
- **Access Management**: Implement role-based access control (RBAC) and the principle of least privilege, where users only have access to the data and systems necessary

for their work.

- **Data Encryption**: Encrypt data in transit and at rest to prevent unauthorized access. Use secure protocols like HTTPS for online communications.
- **Multi-Factor Authentication (MFA)**: Strengthen account security with multi-factor authentication, combining something the user knows (password) with something they possess (token, smartphone).
- **Updates and Patches**: Keep all software, operating systems, and applications up to date with the latest security patches to close known vulnerabilities.

Solutions for Continuous Data Protection

In addition to implementing best practices, it is crucial to adopt advanced solutions for continuous data and system protection:

- **Antivirus and Anti-Malware**: Use antivirus and anti-malware software to detect, block, and remove malicious software. Ensure these tools are up to date and perform regular scans.
- **Threat Monitoring and Analysis**: Deploy continuous monitoring systems to detect abnormal behavior and signs of intrusion. Security Information and Event Management (SIEM) tools can help centralize and analyze activity logs.
- **Regular Backups**: Perform regular and automated backups of all critical data. Store backup copies in secure locations and regularly test recovery procedures to ensure they work properly.
- **Incident Response Plans**: Develop and document incident response plans to react quickly in case of a cyberattack. Ensure staff are familiar with the procedures to follow and that clear communication mechanisms are in place.
- **Security Training**: Organize regular cybersecurity training to raise employee awareness of common threats and best practices. Encourage a culture of vigilance and compliance within the company.

Compliance with Regulations

Data protection is not only about technical security; it also includes compliance with regulations governing data management:

- **GDPR (General Data Protection Regulation):** If your SME collects or processes personal data of individuals residing in the EU, ensure compliance with GDPR requirements, including individual rights, security obligations, and transparency standards.
- **HIPAA (Health Insurance Portability and Accountability Act):** For companies operating in the healthcare sector, compliance with HIPAA standards is essential to protect patient health information.
- **PCI DSS (Payment Card Industry Data Security Standard):** If you manage credit card transactions, you must comply with PCI DSS standards to ensure the security of payment information.

By implementing robust IT security and data protection measures, your SME can defend against cyber threats, protect sensitive information, and ensure operational continuity. Additionally, compliance with data protection regulations strengthens customer trust and business relationships, ensuring the longevity and success of your business in the digital age.

CHAPTER 6: DIGITIZING BUSINESS PROCESSES

With the right technologies in place, the next step is to digitize your business processes to maximize efficiency and reduce costs. Automating repetitive tasks and optimizing processes can transform how your business operates daily. In this chapter, we will explore how to use AI to enhance productivity and present concrete examples of successful digitization in finance, marketing, and human resources.

6.1 Automating Repetitive Tasks and Optimizing Processes

Automating repetitive tasks and optimizing processes are key elements in improving operational efficiency and reducing costs in an SME. By leveraging automation, businesses can free up time and resources to focus on higher-value activities.

Identifying Tasks to Automate

To maximize the benefits of automation, it's essential to identify the processes and tasks best suited for automation.

- **Repetitive and Low-Value Tasks**: Activities that are frequently repeated and do not require complex human intervention are ideal for automation. This includes data entry, order processing, and database updates.
- **Rule-Based Processes**: Processes that follow specific rules or procedures can be automated with systems capable of executing these rules systematically.
- **Tasks Requiring High Accuracy**: Tasks where human errors can have significant consequences, such as accounting and inventory management, are well-suited for automation to improve accuracy.

Automation Tools and Technologies

Various tools and technologies enable the automation of repetitive tasks and process optimization in an SME.

- **Robotic Process Automation (RPA)**: RPA software uses software robots to automate repetitive and routine tasks. They can mimic human actions on user interfaces, such as clicks, data entry, and system navigation.
  - **Examples**: UiPath, Blue Prism, Automation Anywhere.
- **Scripts and Macros**: Scripts and macros are simple programs designed to automate specific tasks in common applications like Excel or database management systems.
  - **Examples**: VBA for Excel, SQL scripts for automating queries.

- **Workflow Automation Tools**: Workflow automation tools help orchestrate and automate complex business processes by linking multiple systems and applications.
  - **Examples**: Make, Zapier, Microsoft Power Automate, Nintex.
- **Chatbots and Virtual Assistants**: These tools automate interactions with customers and employees, especially for common queries or technical support.
  - **Examples**: Chatfuel, Tars, IBM Watson Assistant.
- **Automated Content Management Systems (CMS)**: Automated CMS manage and publish digitized content without constant human intervention.
  - **Examples**: WordPress with automation plugins, Contentful.

Steps to Implement Automation

Implementing automation must be carefully planned to ensure project success and maximize benefits.

1. **Analyze Existing Processes**:
   - Map out current processes to identify friction points, inefficiencies, and opportunities for automation.
   - Prioritize processes based on their frequency, complexity, and potential impact on the business.
2. **Select Automation Tools**:
   - Choose appropriate technologies and tools based on the specific needs of your SME and the processes identified for automation.
   - Consider criteria such as ease of integration, user-friendliness, and cost.
3. **Development and Testing**:
   - Develop automated workflows and test them in controlled environments to validate their effectiveness.
   - Involve key users in testing to gather feedback

and refine the solutions.

4. **Gradual Deployment:**
   - Deploy automation in phases, starting with less critical processes to minimize risks.
   - Monitor performance and adjust settings as needed to optimize results.

5. **Training and Organizational Change:**
   - Train employees on the use of new tools and the monitoring of automated processes.
   - Adopt a change management strategy to facilitate the acceptance and integration of automation into the corporate culture.

6. **Evaluation and Continuous Improvement:**
   - Track key performance indicators (KPIs) to assess the impact of automation on efficiency, quality, and operational costs.
   - Continue exploring new automation opportunities and adjust existing processes to maximize long-term benefits.

By automating repetitive tasks and optimizing processes, your SME can gain efficiency, reduce costs, and improve the accuracy and quality of operations. This also frees up time and resources to focus on strategic and high-value initiatives.

6.2 Using AI to Enhance Productivity

Artificial Intelligence (AI) offers revolutionary capabilities to improve SME productivity. By automating complex tasks, providing deep insights, and offering intelligent solutions, AI can transform how businesses operate. This subchapter explores practical AI applications to enhance productivity and provides concrete examples of implementation.

Practical AI Applications in SMEs

AI can be applied to various operational areas to improve efficiency and decision-making.

- **Robotic Process Automation (RPA) with AI**: RPA solutions integrated with AI can automate more complex tasks that require decision-making. For example, AI can analyze documents, extract relevant information, and make decisions based on predefined rules.
    - **Example**: Automating invoice processing, where AI recognizes and extracts data from scanned invoices, validates information, and initiates payments.
- **Predictive Analytics**: Use machine learning algorithms to analyze historical data and predict future trends. This enables SMEs to make data-driven decisions, optimize inventories, and plan resources more effectively.
    - **Example**: Demand forecasting based on past sales and market trends to optimize inventory management.
- **Customer Service with Chatbots and Virtual Assistants**: AI-powered chatbots can handle customer inquiries continuously and instantly, improving customer experience while reducing the workload of support teams.
    - **Example**: A chatbot on the company's website helps customers find information, place orders, or resolve common issues without human

intervention.

- **Personalization of Marketing Offers**: AI can analyze customer behavior and segment the audience to create personalized and targeted marketing campaigns, increasing conversion rates and customer satisfaction.
  - ◦ **Example**: Using AI to personalize newsletters based on customers' preferences and purchase history.
- **Optimizing Recruitment Processes**: AI tools can analyze resumes, shortlist candidates, and even conduct virtual interviews, making the recruitment process faster and more efficient.
  - ◦ **Example**: Analyzing received resumes to identify candidates who best match the job criteria.

Examples of Productivity Improvement

The following concrete examples illustrate how AI can improve productivity in an SME:

- **Automating Email Processing**: AI can automatically classify and respond to certain emails, reducing the time employees spend sorting emails and allowing for more efficient communication management.
  - ◦ **Example**: An AI system filters emails based on their content and routes them to the appropriate departments or generates automatic responses for common requests.
- **Smart Supply Chain Management**: AI solutions can optimize the supply chain by predicting stockouts, identifying top-performing suppliers, and optimizing inventory levels to reduce costs and lead times.
  - ◦ **Example**: Using AI to forecast production needs and adjust raw material orders accordingly.
- **Automated IT Support**: Virtual assistants and AI systems can provide first-level technical support, diagnose common issues, and offer instant solutions.
  - ◦ **Example**: A virtual assistant helps employees

resolve common IT issues such as password resets or software configurations.

Steps to Integrate AI into Your SME

To leverage AI and improve productivity, follow these steps:

1. **Identify Use Cases**:
   - Evaluate current processes to identify areas where AI can bring significant improvements. Focus on repetitive tasks, data-driven decision-making processes, and areas requiring customer interactions.

2. **Select Tools and Partners**:
   - Choose AI solutions that meet your specific needs. Collaborate with technology providers and expert partners to ensure effective implementation.

3. **Data Collection and Preparation**:
   - Ensure access to relevant, high-quality data that will feed AI models. Data quality is crucial for obtaining accurate and useful predictions.

4. **Development and Testing**:
   - Develop AI models tailored to your needs and test them in a pilot environment to evaluate their performance and impact. Involve your teams early on to adjust parameters and optimize results.

5. **Deployment and Training**:
   - Deploy AI solutions company-wide and train employees on their use. Ensure that staff understand the benefits of AI and know how to use it effectively.

6. **Monitoring and Continuous Improvement**:
   - Track the performance of AI solutions using specific KPIs. Gather user feedback and iterate on the models to continuously improve them.

By integrating AI into your SME's processes, you can revolutionize how you work, improve productivity, and increase competitiveness. This allows you to free up human resources for higher-value tasks while providing intelligent and effective solutions to your operational challenges.

6.3 Examples of Successful Digitization in Finance, Marketing, and HR

Digitization offers unique opportunities to transform operations in various areas of a business. By adopting digital technologies, SMEs can improve efficiency, accuracy, and customer satisfaction. This subchapter presents concrete examples of successful digitization in finance, marketing, and human resources (HR).

Finance

Digitization in finance enables more transparent, efficient, and accurate management of a company's financial resources.

- **Automating Accounting**: Using automated accounting software, SMEs can simplify accounting processes, reduce costs, and minimize human errors.
  - **Example**: An SME adopts software like QuickBooks to automate invoice entry, bank reconciliation, and financial reporting. Accountants can then focus on financial analysis and strategy rather than repetitive tasks.
- **Managing Payments and Invoicing**: Online payment platforms and electronic invoicing solutions reduce the time and effort required to manage transactions.
  - **Example**: By using Stripe for online payments and Zoho Invoice for electronic invoicing, an SME can speed up billing cycles, improve cash flow, and provide a better customer experience.
- **Real-Time Financial Analysis**: Business intelligence tools allow tracking financial performance in real-time and quickly identifying trends and anomalies.
  - **Example**: An SME uses Power BI to create interactive dashboards and visualize key financial indicators, enabling managers to make more informed and timely decisions.

Marketing

Digital marketing transforms how businesses reach and interact with their customers, offering more efficient and measurable ways to promote products and services.

- **Automated Email Marketing**: Automated email marketing platforms allow personalized communications and targeted lead nurturing.
  - ○ **Example**: Using Mailchimp, an SME creates segmented email campaigns based on user behavior, increasing conversion rates and customer loyalty.
- **Online Advertising Campaigns**: Social media and search engine ad management tools offer a targeted and measurable way to promote products.
  - ○ **Example**: With Google Ads and Facebook Ads, an SME can launch targeted advertising campaigns based on user demographics and interests, optimizing advertising ROI.
- **Marketing Performance Analysis**: Marketing analytics platforms provide detailed insights into campaign effectiveness and customer behavior.
  - ○ **Example**: Using Google Analytics to track website traffic, measure user engagement, and analyze conversions, allowing for the adjustment of marketing strategies based on data.

Human Resources (HR)

Digitizing HR processes improves the efficiency of personnel management, payroll, recruitment, and performance.

- **Human Resource Information Systems (HRIS)**: HRIS centralizes all aspects of personnel management, payroll, and benefits, reducing administrative tasks and improving data accuracy.
  - ○ **Example**: An SME implements BambooHR to manage employee records, track leave, and administer benefits, simplifying administrative processes and enhancing employee engagement.
- **Online Recruitment and Onboarding**: Recruitment and

onboarding platforms streamline the hiring process from job posting to new employee integration.

- ○ **Example**: Using LinkedIn Recruiter to find and engage talent, followed by using Workable's onboarding tool to integrate new employees in a structured and efficient manner.
- **Performance Evaluation and Training**: Performance evaluation systems and online training platforms create an environment conducive to employee growth and development.
  - ○ **Example**: An SME uses ClearCompany for continuous performance evaluations and platforms like Coursera to offer ongoing training to employees, ensuring constant professional development.

By adopting digital solutions in finance, marketing, and human resources, SMEs can not only improve the efficiency and accuracy of operations but also strengthen their ability to respond quickly to market changes and customer needs. These examples illustrate how digital technologies can transform and optimize internal processes, offering significant competitive advantages.

CHAPTER 7: ENGAGING CUSTOMERS IN THE DIGITAL AGE

A successful digital transformation is incomplete without solid customer engagement. Digital tools offer unprecedented opportunities to enhance the customer experience and build customer loyalty. This chapter focuses on strategies to engage customers in the digital age, using tools like CRM, omnichannel solutions, and optimizing customer relationship management to create personalized and effective experiences.

7.1 Enhancing the Customer Experience with Digital Tools

Customer experience is a critical factor in customer loyalty and satisfaction. Digital tools offer numerous opportunities to improve this experience by making interactions smoother, more personalized, and efficient. This subchapter explores how SMEs can use various digital tools to transform the customer experience.

Tools for Better Customer Relationship Management (CRM)

Customer Relationship Management (CRM) systems centralize customer information and facilitate the management of customer interactions and data.

- **Personalizing Interactions**: A CRM system allows you to track each customer's preferences, purchase history, and past interactions. SMEs can thus personalize their communications and offers.
  - **Example**: Using Salesforce to send product recommendations based on previous purchases and customer interests.
- **Automating Processes**: CRM tools automate tasks such as sending follow-up emails, managing leads, and segmenting customer data, improving efficiency and responsiveness.
  - **Example**: HubSpot CRM for automating welcome and thank-you emails, thereby enhancing customer engagement from the first interaction.

Omnichannel Experience

Providing a consistent and seamless customer experience across all communication channels is essential to meet modern customer expectations.

- **Channel Integration**: Ensure that customer interactions are integrated and tracked across all channels (email, chat, phone, social media) to provide a continuous and seamless experience.

- **Example**: Using Zendesk to centralize customer interactions from various channels and offer consistent and prompt support.
- **Advanced E-Commerce Platforms**: E-commerce platforms can offer personalized shopping experiences, product recommendations, and simplified checkout processes.
  - **Example**: Shopify allows customizing the storefront based on visitor behavior, offering product suggestions, and streamlining checkout for an optimized shopping experience.

Real-Time Feedback and Interaction

Collecting real-time feedback and proactively interacting with customers help continuously improve the customer experience.

- **Customer Feedback Tools**: Use online surveys, questionnaires, and feedback tools to gather customer opinions on their experiences and identify areas for improvement.
  - **Example**: SurveyMonkey to send post-purchase surveys and gather feedback on customer satisfaction and suggestions for improvement.
- **Live Chat and Chatbots**: Live chat tools and chatbots can provide instant assistance, answer frequently asked questions, and resolve issues in real-time, enhancing customer satisfaction.
  - **Example**: Intercom for offering real-time assistance to website visitors, improving the accessibility and responsiveness of customer service.

Personalization and Engagement

Personalizing the customer experience and proactive engagement strengthen customer loyalty and satisfaction.

- **Content Personalization**: Content management systems (CMS) and analytics tools allow you to personalize content based on user behaviors and preferences.
  - **Example**: Using WordPress with

personalization plugins to display specific content and offers based on user browsing behavior.

- **Digital Loyalty Programs**: Loyalty platforms can incentivize repeat customers by offering rewards, discounts, and exclusive benefits.
  - ◦ **Example**: Using Smile.io to create and manage loyalty programs, offering points and rewards for repeat purchases, referrals, and social media interactions.

Importance of User Experience (UX)

A well-designed user experience (UX) is crucial for maximizing engagement and conversions.

- **User-Centered Design**: Adopt a user-centered design approach by developing intuitive interfaces and facilitating navigation.
  - ◦ **Example**: Using UX design techniques to test and improve user journeys on the website, reducing friction and increasing conversion rates.
- **Mobile Optimization**: With the rise of mobile users, it's essential to optimize websites and apps to provide a smooth and responsive experience across all devices.
  - ◦ **Example**: Using Google AMP to speed up page loading times on mobile devices, ensuring a fast and pleasant experience for mobile users.

By using digital tools to improve the customer experience, SMEs can not only meet the growing expectations of customers but also strengthen their loyalty and engagement. A customer-centered approach, supported by advanced technologies, enables more personalized, responsive, and satisfying interactions, contributing to the long-term growth and success of the business.

7.2 Digital Marketing Strategies (SEO, Social Media, Email Marketing)

Digital marketing is essential for attracting, engaging, and converting customers online. Strategies like search engine optimization (SEO), social media campaigns, and email marketing allow SMEs to reach a broader audience in an effective and measurable way.

Search Engine Optimization (SEO)

SEO is crucial for improving your website's visibility on search engines like Google. Better visibility translates to increased organic traffic, which can lead to more conversion opportunities without high advertising costs.

- **Keyword Research**: Identify relevant keywords that your target audience uses to search for products or services similar to yours. Use tools like Google Keyword Planner, SEMrush, or Ahrefs to discover these keywords.
  - **Example**: For an SME selling gardening products, relevant keywords might include "gardening tools," "organic garden plants," and "garden maintenance tips."
- **On-Page Optimization**: Optimize elements of your website such as title tags, meta descriptions, headers, and content for targeted keywords. Ensure that your content is high-quality and meets user needs.
  - **Example**: Writing informative blog posts on topics related to gardening using identified keywords, such as "How to Choose the Best Gardening Tools for Beginners."
- **Off-Page Optimization**: Acquire quality backlinks from authoritative websites in your field. Backlinks enhance your site's credibility in the eyes of search engines.
  - **Example**: Collaborating with influential bloggers in the gardening niche to get links to your site or contributing guest posts to relevant sites.

Social Media

Social media platforms are powerful tools for reaching a broad audience, building a community, and interacting directly with customers.

- **Platform Selection**: Choose the social media platforms that best align with your target audience and business goals, such as Facebook, Instagram, LinkedIn, Twitter, and Pinterest.
  - **Example**: An SME in the fashion industry might choose Instagram and Pinterest to showcase products through visually appealing content.
- **Creating Engaging Content**: Produce diverse and engaging content, including images, videos, infographics, and articles. The content should be relevant and interesting to your target audience.
  - **Example**: Posting video tutorials on Instagram showing how to style fashion items or creating photo albums on Facebook for new seasonal collections.
- **Targeted Advertising**: Use targeted advertising options on social media to reach specific segments of your audience. Social media ads allow targeting users based on demographics, behaviors, and interests.
  - **Example**: Using Facebook Ads to promote a new product line and target users interested in fashion who have recently visited clothing retail websites.
- **Engagement and Interaction**: Encourage interaction with your posts, respond to comments and messages, and create polls or contests to maintain high engagement.
  - **Example**: Hosting an Instagram contest asking participants to share photos of their favorite outfits featuring your product, with a prize for the best photo.

Email Marketing

Email marketing is a powerful tool for reaching customers directly, nurturing leads, and retaining existing customers.

- **List Segmentation**: Segment your contact list based on criteria like purchase behaviors, interests, location, and past interactions. This allows you to send personalized and relevant messages.
  - **Example**: An SME selling sports gear might segment its list based on the sports customers engage in (e.g., running, cycling, yoga) and send product recommendations tailored to each segment.
- **Personalized Content**: Create personalized email campaigns with content tailored to the interests and needs of each segment. Use attractive visuals and clear calls to action.
  - **Example**: Sending newsletters with training tips, product recommendations, and special promotions based on customers' previous purchases.
- **Email Automation**: Use automation tools to send emails triggered by specific user actions, such as signing up for a newsletter, abandoning a cart, or making a recent purchase.
  - **Example**: Setting up an automated welcome email series for new subscribers, introducing the company's story, popular products, and offering a welcome discount.
- **Performance Analysis**: Track and analyze key metrics such as open rates, click-through rates, and conversions to evaluate the effectiveness of your email marketing campaigns and adjust your strategy accordingly.
  - **Example**: Using performance reports to identify which email campaigns have the highest conversion rates and refining future sends to maximize engagement and sales.

By implementing effective digital marketing strategies such as SEO, social media campaigns, and email marketing, SMEs can reach a broader audience, engage customers meaningfully, and increase conversion rates. These approaches help build stronger connections with customers, increase brand awareness, and drive sales growth in an ever-evolving digital landscape.

7.3 Using Customer Data to Personalize Offers

Collecting and analyzing customer data allows businesses to better understand consumer needs, preferences, and behaviors. With these insights, SMEs can personalize their offers, enhance customer engagement, and increase conversions. This subchapter explores methods for collecting and using customer data to deliver personalized offers.

Collecting Customer Data

To personalize offers, it is essential to have accurate and comprehensive customer data. Here are some sources for data collection:

- **Sign-Up Forms and Surveys**: Use sign-up forms and surveys to gather demographic information, preferences, and interests from customers.
  - **Example**: Ask customers to fill out a short questionnaire when signing up for a newsletter or creating an online account to learn about their interests and preferences.
- **Transaction History**: Analyze previous purchase data to identify favorite products, purchase frequencies, and amounts spent.
  - **Example**: Use order history data to determine frequently purchased items and offer bundled deals or targeted discounts.
- **Online Behavior**: Monitor browsing behaviors on the website, such as pages visited, products viewed, and time spent.
  - **Example**: Use Google Analytics to track user journeys on the site and identify the most popular products, then recommend similar items.
- **Social Media Interactions**: Analyze customer interactions on social media, including likes, shares, and comments, to better understand their interests and preferences.

- **Example**: Use Facebook Insights data to identify the most engaging posts and tailor marketing campaigns accordingly.

Analyzing Customer Data

Once data is collected, it must be analyzed to extract actionable insights.

- **Customer Segmentation**: Segment your customer database into distinct groups based on criteria such as purchase behaviors, product preferences, and demographic characteristics.
  - **Example**: Segment customers by purchase frequency (regular, occasional, new customers) and create specific marketing campaigns for each segment.
- **Predictive Analysis**: Use machine learning algorithms to predict future customer behaviors, such as the likelihood of purchasing a product or the probability of churn.
  - **Example**: Use a predictive model to identify customers likely to unsubscribe and offer them incentives to retain their loyalty.
- **Customer Journey Mapping**: Analyze the customer journey from the first interaction with the company to purchase and beyond to identify friction points and personalization opportunities.
  - **Example**: Use customer journey mapping tools to visualize key stages and optimize each touchpoint based on the customer's specific needs.

Personalizing Offers

Leveraging customer data allows you to create personalized offers that meet the specific expectations and preferences of each customer.

- **Product Recommendations**: Use recommendation systems to suggest products based on customers' preferences and purchase behaviors.

- **Example**: Use a recommendation engine to display similar or complementary products on the product page or in follow-up emails, similar to Amazon's approach.
- **Personalized Email Campaigns**: Send targeted and relevant emails based on customer segments and behavioral data.
  - **Example**: Send reminder emails to customers who have abandoned their cart, offering a special discount to complete their purchase.
- **Special Offers and Promotions**: Create special offers and promotions based on customers' purchase history and preferences to increase engagement and sales.
  - **Example**: Offer exclusive discounts on customers' favorite products or organize private sales for the most loyal customer segments.
- **Web Content Personalization**: Adjust website content in real-time for each visitor based on their preferences and past behaviors.
  - **Example**: Use personalization plugins to display banners, special offers, or recommended content based on pages previously visited by the customer.

Measurement and Optimization

To ensure the effectiveness of personalization, it is crucial to measure results and optimize accordingly.

- **Key Performance Indicators (KPIs)**: Track specific KPIs such as conversion rate, average order value, and customer retention to assess the impact of personalization strategies.
  - **Example**: Analyze sales increases following the implementation of personalized product recommendations.
- **Customer Feedback**: Collect customer feedback to understand their satisfaction and identify areas for improvement.
  - **Example**: Use post-purchase surveys to gather

opinions on product recommendations and email marketing campaigns.

- **A/B Testing**: Conduct A/B tests to compare different versions of personalized campaigns and determine which generates the best results.
  - ◦ **Example**: Test different variants of abandoned cart reminder emails to identify the most effective offer or message.

By using customer data to personalize offers, SMEs can improve the customer experience, increase engagement, and maximize conversions. Data-driven personalization strengthens customer loyalty and creates a closer, more meaningful relationship with each customer, laying the foundation for sustainable growth and a strong competitive advantage.

CHAPTER 8: MONITORING AND EVALUATING PROGRESS

After implementing digital technologies and digitizing your business processes, it is crucial to monitor and evaluate the progress made to ensure the success of your digital transformation. Measuring and analyzing your performance allows you to understand what works, identify areas for improvement, and make informed decisions for the future. This chapter discusses the tools and techniques for monitoring and evaluation, as well as the key performance indicators (KPIs) to track to measure the impact of your digital initiatives.

8.1 Key Performance Indicators (KPIs) for Digital Transformation

Digital transformation is a complex process that requires continuous evaluation to ensure its success. Key performance indicators (KPIs) are essential metrics for measuring the effectiveness of digital initiatives, tracking progress, and identifying areas needing improvement. This subchapter explores the main KPIs to monitor for evaluating your SME's digital transformation.

Choosing the Right KPIs

To effectively measure digital transformation, it is crucial to select KPIs that align with your company's specific goals. Here are some categories of KPIs to consider:

- **Operational Performance KPIs:**
  - **Employee Productivity**: Measure employee productivity before and after implementing digital technologies. This can include the number of tasks completed, the average time to complete a task, and the rate of process automation.
    - **Example**: Track the average order processing time before and after automating order management systems.
- **Financial KPIs:**
  - **Return on Investment (ROI)**: Calculate the ROI of digital transformation projects by comparing the financial gains achieved with the costs incurred.
    - **Example**: Calculate the ROI of implementing a CRM by measuring the increase in sales and the reduction in operational costs.
- **Customer Satisfaction KPIs:**
  - **Net Promoter Score (NPS)**: Measure customer satisfaction and loyalty using NPS surveys to

evaluate customers' willingness to recommend your company.

- **Example**: Track NPS after implementing new customer support technologies like chatbots.

- **Technical Performance KPIs**:
  - **System Availability**: Monitor the availability and reliability of IT systems to ensure they operate without interruption.
    - **Example**: Measure cloud service uptime and the resolution rate of technical issues.

How to Measure and Interpret Results

Once KPIs are defined, it's important to set up mechanisms to regularly measure and interpret the results. Here are some methods to achieve this:

- **Dashboards and Reports**:
  - **Data Centralization**: Use dashboard tools to centralize data from various KPIs and visualize performance in real-time.
    - **Example**: Use Microsoft Power BI or Tableau to create interactive dashboards that display trends and deviations from goals.

- **Periodic Analysis**:
  - **Performance Review**: Hold regular meetings to review performance and discuss results with key stakeholders.
    - **Example**: Hold quarterly meetings to assess digital transformation progress and adjust strategies accordingly.

- **Benchmarking**:
  - **Comparison with Standards**: Compare your KPIs with industry benchmarks to assess how your company stands against competitors.
    - **Example**: Use analyst reports or market studies to compare your company's NPS

with the industry average.

- **Gap Analysis**:
  - **Identifying Gaps**: Analyze the gaps between actual performance and set goals to identify areas needing improvement.
    - **Example**: Measure the gap between targeted order processing time and actual processing time to identify inefficiencies.

Examples of Digital Transformation-Specific KPIs

Here are some concrete examples of KPIs to monitor as part of a digital transformation:

- **Technology Adoption Rate**:
  - **Description**: Percentage of users adopting new technologies compared to the total number of targeted users.
  - **Utility**: Measure the success of implementation and the acceptance of new technologies by employees.
- **Automation Rate**:
  - **Description**: Percentage of business processes that have been automated compared to the total number of processes identified for automation.
  - **Utility**: Evaluate the effectiveness of automation in reducing manual tasks and improving operational efficiency.
- **First Contact Resolution Rate**:
  - **Description**: Percentage of customer support requests resolved during the first contact with the customer service team.
  - **Utility**: Measure the effectiveness of digital customer support tools and customer satisfaction.
- **Time to Deploy New Technologies**:
  - **Description**: Average time required to deploy new technologies or updates.
  - **Utility**: Assess how quickly the company can

implement technological changes and adapt to market shifts.

By choosing relevant KPIs and setting up effective processes to measure and interpret results, your SME can track progress in digital transformation and adjust strategies accordingly. This ensures that objectives are met and that digital initiatives provide tangible value to the business.

8.2 Methods for Evaluating and Analyzing Results

Evaluating and analyzing results is essential for understanding the impact of digital transformation initiatives and making necessary adjustments. Implementing effective methods not only measures success but also detects areas needing improvement. This subchapter explores various methods for evaluating and analyzing the results of digital transformation.

Continuous Evaluation

Continuous evaluation involves regularly monitoring and measuring performance, allowing for the quick identification of issues and the adjustment of strategies.

- **Periodic KPI Review**:
  - **Description**: Hold regular reviews of key performance indicators (KPIs) to analyze progress against set goals.
  - **Example**: Hold monthly meetings to review performance in productivity, ROI, customer satisfaction, and other relevant KPIs.
- **Internal Audits**:
  - **Description**: Conduct regular internal audits to ensure that processes and technologies are being used and optimized correctly.
  - **Example**: Conduct quarterly audits to assess the compliance of IT security practices with established standards.
- **Stakeholder Feedback**:
  - **Description**: Continuously collect feedback from employees, customers, and partners to evaluate the impact of digital changes.
  - **Example**: Use surveys and interviews to gather feedback on new technologies and their impact on daily operations.

Techniques for Analyzing Results

Once data is collected, it's crucial to analyze it thoroughly to extract actionable insights.

- **Trend Analysis**:
  - **Description**: Analyze trends from collected data to identify patterns and changes over time.
  - **Example**: Analyze seasonal sales trends over several years to anticipate peak demand periods and adjust marketing strategies.
- **Benchmarking**:
  - **Description**: Compare your company's performance against industry leaders or industry standards.
  - **Example**: Compare your company's customer satisfaction scores with those of competitors to identify areas for improvement.
- **SWOT Analysis**:
  - **Description**: Use SWOT analysis (Strengths, Weaknesses, Opportunities, Threats) to evaluate the impact of digital transformation.
  - **Example**: Identify strengths such as increased productivity, weaknesses like the learning curve, and adjust plans accordingly.

Advanced Analysis Models

To go further in evaluating impacts, consider advanced analysis models that use statistical techniques and artificial intelligence technologies.

- **Predictive Analysis**:
  - **Description**: Use machine learning algorithms to predict future outcomes based on past and current trends.
  - **Example**: Predict future sales based on historical sales data, market trends, and customer behavior.
- **Root Cause Analysis**:
  - **Description**: Identify the underlying causes of performance gaps to determine necessary corrective actions.
  - **Example**: Use Pareto or Ishikawa diagrams to analyze the reasons for project delivery delays.

- **Sentiment Analysis**:
  - ◦ **Description**: Use sentiment analysis tools on social media data and customer reviews to understand customer sentiment towards your products or services.
  - ◦ **Example**: Analyze social media comments to detect signs of customer dissatisfaction or satisfaction.

Reporting and Data Visualization

Clearly presenting results is essential for informed decision-making. Use data visualization tools to create compelling reports.

- **Interactive Dashboards**:
  - ◦ **Description**: Create interactive dashboards to visualize performance and enable dynamic analysis.
  - ◦ **Example**: Use Microsoft Power BI to develop dashboards that display KPIs in real-time, with filters to zoom in on specific details.
- **Automated Reports**:
  - ◦ **Description**: Set up automated reports for regular and timely updates on critical KPIs.
  - ◦ **Example**: Configure automated weekly reports generated by Google Analytics to track website and marketing campaign performance.
- **Data Storytelling**:
  - ◦ **Description**: Use storytelling to contextualize data and tell a compelling story about the impacts of digital transformation.
  - ◦ **Example**: Prepare presentations for management meetings highlighting not only numbers but also success stories and lessons learned.

Adjusting Strategy

Based on the analysis, adjust digital transformation strategies to optimize results and ensure objectives are met.

- **Reevaluating Objectives**:
  - ◦ **Description**: Adjust objectives based on the

progress made and new insights gathered.

- ◦ **Example**: Revise annual sales growth goals after seeing faster-than-expected increases in online sales.
- **Adapting Processes and Technologies**:
    - ◦ **Description**: Modify business processes and technologies used to improve their efficiency and alignment with strategic goals.
    - ◦ **Example**: Implement new features in the CRM following positive feedback from sales teams on productivity improvements.
- **Resource Allocation**:
    - ◦ **Description**: Reallocate resources based on priorities identified during analysis, optimizing the use of human, financial, and technological resources.
    - ◦ **Example**: Allocate more budget to high-performing digital marketing campaigns after observing an increase in ROI.

By adopting rigorous methods for evaluating and analyzing the results of digital transformation, SMEs can ensure that their initiatives deliver expected benefits and align with strategic objectives. This allows for informed decision-making, maximizes return on investment, and continuously adjusts strategies to adapt to emerging challenges and opportunities.

CHAPTER 9: PRACTICAL CASES AND CASE STUDIES

After exploring the various strategies and tools necessary for digital transformation, it is both inspiring and instructive to see how other SMEs have successfully navigated their own digitalization journeys. By examining examples and case studies, you can discover practical approaches and innovative ideas that you can adapt to your own business. This chapter presents a series of testimonials and detailed examples to illustrate the successes and challenges faced by different SMEs in their digital transformation.

9.1 Examples of SMEs that Successfully Achieved Digital Transformation

Testimonials from SMEs that have successfully undergone digital transformation offer valuable insights and serve as inspiration for other companies seeking digitalization. Below is a series of testimonials from SMEs across different sectors that have leveraged digital technologies to transform their operations and achieve remarkable results.

Testimonial 1: An SME in the Healthcare Sector

Company Name: Medico Santé

Context: Medico Santé, an SME specializing in the distribution of medical equipment, faced increased competition and struggled with stock management and product availability.

Digital Transformation Initiatives:

- **ERP Implementation:** Medico Santé adopted an ERP system to centralize stock, order, and finance management.
- **Process Automation:** The company automated order processing and stock management to reduce errors and delays.
- **E-commerce Platform:** A new e-commerce platform was implemented to facilitate online orders and improve the customer experience.

Results:

- **30% Reduction in Order Errors:** Automation significantly reduced errors, increasing customer satisfaction.
- **Improved Stock Management:** The ERP system provided real-time stock visibility, reducing stockouts and surpluses.
- **50% Increase in Online Sales:** The new e-commerce platform attracted more customers and streamlined the ordering process.

Testimonial 2: An SME in the Fashion Industry

Company Name: Style Chic

Context: Style Chic, an SME in the fashion industry, sought to increase visibility and customer loyalty amidst the rise of competing online stores.

Digital Transformation Initiatives:

- **SEO and Digital Marketing:** The company launched an SEO and digital marketing strategy to drive more traffic to its website.
- **Social Media Utilization:** Style Chic enhanced its presence on Instagram and Facebook to promote collections and engage with customers.
- **CRM for Personalization:** Implementing a CRM allowed for personalized offers and marketing campaigns based on customer purchasing behavior.

Results:

- **60% Increase in Website Traffic:** Thanks to SEO and digital marketing campaigns, Style Chic's website saw a significant rise in visitors.
- **Increased Social Media Engagement:** Followers and interactions on Instagram and Facebook grew, strengthening brand awareness.
- **Improved Customer Loyalty:** The CRM enabled personalized communications, boosting customer satisfaction and loyalty.

Testimonial 3: An SME in the Manufacturing Sector

Company Name: TechFab

Context: TechFab, an SME specializing in the manufacturing of technical components, faced productivity challenges and issues with meeting delivery deadlines.

Digital Transformation Initiatives:

- **Production Line Automation:** TechFab invested in industrial robots and automated systems to improve production efficiency.
- **IoT Data Analytics:** Integrating IoT sensors allowed real-time data collection on machine performance and production conditions.

- **Optimized Order Management:** A new order management software was implemented to better plan and track orders.

Results:
- **40% Increase in Productivity:** Automation of production lines significantly improved operational efficiency.
- **Reduced Machine Downtime:** IoT data analysis enabled predictive maintenance, reducing downtime and repair costs.
- **On-Time Delivery:** The order management software optimized planning, ensuring delivery deadlines were met.

Testimonial 4: An SME in the Education Sector

Company Name: EduLearn

Context: EduLearn, an SME providing online training services, sought to expand its offerings and improve the learning experience for users.

Digital Transformation Initiatives:
- **Online Learning Platform:** EduLearn developed a user-friendly online learning platform accessible via various devices.
- **AI for Recommendations:** AI algorithms were integrated to personalize learning paths by recommending courses and content tailored to each user.
- **Learning Performance Analytics:** Analytical tools were implemented to track learner progress and identify areas needing additional support.

Results:
- **80% Increase in Enrollments:** The new online learning platform attracted a growing number of learners.
- **Improved Learner Satisfaction:** Personalized recommendations and performance tracking increased user engagement and satisfaction.
- **Course Offerings Expanded:** The ability to analyze

learner needs allowed EduLearn to expand its course catalog based on demand.

These testimonials demonstrate that when digital transformation is well-executed, it can lead to significant gains in efficiency, productivity, and customer satisfaction. By drawing inspiration from these examples, other SMEs can identify strategies and solutions tailored to their specific needs and successfully navigate their own digital transformation journeys.

9.2 Analysis of Success Factors and Mistakes to Avoid

Analyzing the success factors and common mistakes in digital transformation initiatives provides valuable lessons and maximizes the chances of success. By reflecting on the testimonials and case studies presented, we can identify the key elements that contributed to the success of digital transformation projects, as well as the pitfalls to avoid.

Success Factors

1. **Clear Vision and Well-Defined Objectives:**
   - A clear vision and precise objectives guide digital transformation efforts and align initiatives with the company's overall strategy.
   - **Example:** Medico Santé set clear goals for improving stock management and reducing order errors, leading to the successful implementation of an ERP system.

2. **Leadership and Stakeholder Engagement:**
   - Strong support and active involvement from leadership and stakeholders are crucial for mobilizing the necessary resources and ensuring the success of digital projects.
   - **Example:** Style Chic benefited from strong leadership engagement in using social media and personalizing customer offers.

3. **Adaptability and Flexibility:**
   - Being ready to adjust plans based on feedback and market changes helps maintain progress toward set goals.
   - **Example:** TechFab adapted its production processes by integrating IoT technologies and automated systems to improve product quality.

4. **Data Utilization and Analytics:**
   - Leveraging data for informed decision-

making and offer personalization enhances the effectiveness of digital strategies.

- **Example:** EduLearn used data analytics to optimize learner outcomes and expand its course offerings.

5. **Continuous Training and Skill Development:**
   - Investing in continuous training and developing employees' digital skills is essential for fostering technology adoption and improving productivity.
   - **Example:** EduLearn trained its teams on using the online learning platform and analytics tools to personalize learning paths.

Mistakes to Avoid

1. **Lack of Preparation and Planning:**
   - Insufficient planning and needs assessment can lead to cost overruns, delays, and implementation failures.
   - **Example:** Implementing a CRM without assessing specific needs and planning user training may result in adoption issues.

2. **Underestimating Resistance to Change:**
   - Failing to anticipate and manage resistance to change can slow down the transformation and reduce expected benefits.
   - **Example:** Ignoring employees' concerns about automation can lead to decreased morale and engagement.

3. **Inadequate Technological Investments:**
   - Investing in unsuitable or under-evaluated technologies can limit the impact of digital initiatives and lead to financial losses.
   - **Example:** Choosing a poorly performing e-commerce platform can harm the customer experience and reduce online sales.

4. **Lack of Ongoing Monitoring and Evaluation:**

- Failing to establish continuous monitoring and evaluation processes can prevent the identification of issues and the adjustment of strategies.
- **Example:** Not using KPIs to evaluate process automation may lead to suboptimal productivity gains.

5. **Lack of Communication and Collaboration:**
   - Organizational silos and poor communication between teams can hinder the success of digital projects.
   - **Example:** A company where marketing and IT teams do not collaborate effectively may miss opportunities for integration and personalization.

Summary of Best Practices

To successfully achieve digital transformation, SMEs should:

- Define a clear vision and precise objectives.
- Ensure leadership and stakeholder engagement.
- Remain adaptable and flexible in response to feedback and changes.
- Leverage data for informed decision-making and offer personalization.
- Invest in continuous training and skill development for employees.
- Plan rigorously and regularly evaluate progress.
- Anticipate and manage resistance to change.
- Choose technologies that meet the specific needs of the business.
- Foster communication and collaboration across teams.

By avoiding common mistakes and relying on these success factors, SMEs can maximize the benefits of their digital transformation initiatives and achieve sustainable and significant results. The testimonials and case studies presented show that companies adopting a proactive and structured approach can successfully navigate the ever-evolving digital landscape.

CHAPTER 10: FUTURE PERSPECTIVES

After examining various practical and strategic aspects of digital transformation, it is important to look toward the future to understand emerging trends and prepare for upcoming technological evolutions. This chapter will focus on the innovations that are continually redefining the digital landscape and provide guidance on how to prepare your SME for these changes. By exploring technological trends and planning proactively, your business can not only adapt but also thrive in a constantly evolving digital environment.

10.1 Emerging Trends in Digital Transformation

Digital transformation is a constantly evolving phenomenon, influenced by rapid technological advancements and changing consumer behaviors. To remain competitive, SMEs must stay attuned to the emerging trends that are shaping the digital landscape. This section explores some of the most significant trends that are redefining digital transformation.

Artificial Intelligence and Machine Learning

Artificial intelligence (AI) and machine learning continue to revolutionize various sectors through their data analysis and automation capabilities.

- **Conversational AI and Chatbots:** AI-powered chatbots and virtual assistants offer 24/7 customer service and support, improving the customer experience and reducing operational costs.
    - *Example:* SMEs use platforms like IBM Watson or Google Dialogflow to create chatbots capable of handling complex queries while providing a seamless user experience.
- **Predictive Analytics:** Machine learning algorithms analyze massive volumes of data to predict future trends, customer behaviors, and optimize marketing and business strategies.
    - *Example:* An SME in the retail sector uses predictive analytics to anticipate consumer trends and adjust inventory accordingly.

The Internet of Things (IoT)

The Internet of Things (IoT) enables businesses to connect physical devices to the internet, collecting and exchanging data to optimize operations.

- **Smart Logistics:** IoT sensors enhance supply chain management by enabling real-time tracking of goods and optimizing logistics.
    - *Example:* A transportation company uses IoT sensors to monitor the temperature of

perishable goods, ensuring their integrity until delivery.
- **Predictive Maintenance:** IoT sensors detect anomalies in industrial equipment, allowing for proactive maintenance and reducing unplanned downtime.
  - *Example:* A manufacturing SME integrates IoT sensors into its machines to predict failures and schedule maintenance before they impact production.

5G Technology

5G technology promises ultra-fast data speeds, minimal latency, and increased connection capacity, paving the way for new applications and services.
- **Enhanced Connectivity:** 5G enables faster and more reliable wireless connectivity, essential for applications like augmented reality (AR) and virtual reality (VR).
  - *Example:* An SME in the real estate industry uses 5G to offer immersive virtual tours of properties remotely, enhancing the experience for potential buyers.
- **Advanced IoT Applications:** 5G supports a greater number of IoT devices connected simultaneously, enabling smart cities and connected factories.
  - *Example:* An energy management company uses 5G to connect thousands of sensors in urban infrastructures, optimizing energy consumption and reducing costs.

Blockchain and Data Security

Blockchain is a decentralized ledger technology that offers increased security and transparency for digital transactions.
- **Secure Transactions:** Blockchain ensures transparency and integrity in transactions by eliminating intermediaries and securing data.
  - *Example:* An SME in the fintech sector uses blockchain to secure financial transactions and smart contracts, ensuring transparent and reliable operations.

- **Product Traceability:** Blockchain enhances product traceability in the supply chain, boosting consumer trust and ensuring quality.
  - *Example:* A food company adopts blockchain to trace product origins from farm to table, ensuring traceability and trust in the supply chain.

Augmented Reality (AR) and Virtual Reality (VR)

AR and VR transform the user experience by offering immersive and engaging interactions.

- **Enhanced Customer Experience:** AR and VR create immersive customer experiences, allowing users to virtually try products or visualize complex configurations.
  - *Example:* A furniture store uses VR to allow customers to visualize furniture in their space before purchase, reducing returns and improving satisfaction.
- **Training and Education:** VR offers immersive training environments to simulate complex scenarios and improve learning outcomes.
  - *Example:* An SME in the healthcare sector uses VR to train medical staff on surgical procedures in a simulated environment.

Intelligent Process Automation (RPA + AI)

Robotic process automation (RPA) combined with artificial intelligence creates systems capable of automating more complex tasks.

- **Business Process Automation:** RPA solutions automate repetitive tasks, while AI adds decision-making capabilities for more complex tasks.
  - *Example:* A financial services company uses intelligent automation to process loan applications more quickly and accurately.

By staying attentive to these emerging trends, SMEs can anticipate technological changes and seize the opportunities they present.

These innovations provide powerful ways to improve operational efficiency, enrich the customer experience, and strengthen competitiveness in a constantly evolving digital market.

10.2 Preparing Your SME for Future Technological Evolutions

To stay ahead and remain competitive, an SME must actively prepare for future technological evolutions. This involves implementing strategies, structures, and practices that will enable the company to quickly adapt and take advantage of new opportunities. This section explores key steps to prepare your SME for emerging innovations and technologies.

Long-Term Planning

Strategic long-term planning is essential for anticipating technological evolutions and aligning the company's goals with future opportunities.

- **Technology Monitoring:**
  - Establish a system for technology monitoring to track innovations and emerging trends in your industry. This may include attending conferences, reading specialized publications, and subscribing to technology newsletters.
    - *Example:* An SME in the healthcare sector monitors new trends in telemedicine and medical technologies to adapt its services.
- **Technology Roadmap:**
  - Develop a technology roadmap that outlines the technologies to be adopted in the short, medium, and long term. Prioritize investments based on the company's needs and the potential impact of the technologies.
    - *Example:* Create a roadmap to gradually integrate AI into customer service operations, followed by adopting blockchain to secure financial transactions.

Organizational Flexibility and Adaptability

Creating a flexible organizational culture and structure enables your company to quickly adapt to technological changes.

- **Innovation Culture:**
    - Foster a culture that encourages innovation, experimentation, and acceptance of change. Encourage employees to propose new ideas and participate in digital transformation initiatives.
        - *Example:* Organize internal hackathons where employees can collaborate on innovative technology projects.
- **Agile Structures:**
    - Adopt agile organizational structures that allow for rapid changes and effective responses to new opportunities. Use agile methodologies like Scrum or Kanban to manage technology projects.
        - *Example:* An SME uses cross-functional teams and development sprints to speed up the deployment of new features on its online platform.

Investment in Skills and Training

Developing your employees' digital skills is crucial to fully exploit new technologies.

- **Continuous Training:**
    - Implement continuous training programs to keep your employees' skills up to date with the latest technologies and digital practices. Use online courses, workshops, and certifications to offer flexible and accessible learning.
        - *Example:* Offer online courses on platforms like Coursera or Udemy to train employees in AI, cybersecurity, or data analysis.
- **Recruiting Technology Talent:**
    - Attract and recruit talent with advanced technological skills to strengthen your team and bring new perspectives. Collaborate with universities and research centers to identify emerging talent.

- *Example:* Recruit experts in data science and machine learning to develop data-driven solutions.

Partnerships and Collaborations

Strategic partnerships and collaborations can accelerate the adoption of new technologies and provide additional resources.

- **Partnerships with Startups:**
  - Collaborate with innovative startups to benefit from their cutting-edge technologies and agile approach. Partnerships can include joint projects, investments, or strategic acquisitions.
    - *Example:* An SME in the food industry collaborates with a startup specializing in vertical farming to adopt sustainable agricultural practices.

- **Innovation Ecosystems:**
  - Participate in innovation ecosystems, such as incubators, accelerators, or technology clusters, to exchange ideas and resources with other industry players.
    - *Example:* Join a technology cluster to access shared infrastructure, mentors, and funding for R&D projects.

Gradual Adoption of Technologies

Adopting technologies gradually and thoughtfully helps minimize risks and maximize benefits.

- **Pilots and Pilot Projects:**
  - Launch pilot projects to test new technologies on a small scale before deploying them more widely. Use the results of the pilots to evaluate performance and adjust strategies.
    - *Example:* An SME tests a predictive analytics tool to optimize inventory at some of its branches before rolling it out company-wide.

- **Feedback and Iteration:**
  - Gather feedback from end users and

continuously improve deployed technologies. Take an iterative approach to refine solutions based on real needs.

- *Example:* Use employee feedback on new project management software to make adjustments and improve the user experience.

By taking proactive steps to prepare for future technological evolutions, SMEs can not only stay competitive but also fully capitalize on the opportunities offered by digital transformation. Strategic planning, a culture of innovation, investments in skills, and judicious collaborations allow SMEs to successfully navigate a constantly evolving technological landscape.

CONCLUSION

Digital transformation is a journey that offers exceptional opportunities for SMEs. When done well, it not only improves operational efficiency and customer satisfaction but also catalyzes innovation and growth. This practical guide has provided the tools, strategies, and concrete examples needed to embark on this journey with confidence and clarity.

From the initial diagnosis of your company's current state to the development of a robust digital strategy, including the crucial importance of corporate culture, continuous training, and the adoption of the right technologies, every step of this process is essential to ensure a successful transformation. The testimonials and case studies demonstrate that, regardless of size or sector, SMEs can derive immense benefit from digitalization.

By staying attentive to emerging trends and preparing for future technological evolutions, SMEs can not only adapt to a constantly evolving environment but also seize new opportunities as they arise. Flexibility, innovation, and proactivity are the key words for successfully navigating the digital universe.

In summary, digital transformation is not an end in itself but a powerful means to achieve strategic objectives and ensure the sustainability and prosperity of your business. As you move forward in this process, continue to learn, experiment, and adapt, as this is how you will fully harness the potential of digitalization.
Happy digital transformation!

www.ingramcontent.com/pod-product-compliance
Lightning Source LLC
Chambersburg PA
CBHW071945210526
45479CB00002B/823

* 9 7 9 8 3 3 5 5 9 4 2 5 7 *